WHISPERING WIND

*Tsohanoai came and poured water through the top of
the sweat-house on the stones*

WHISPERING WIND

Folktales of the Navaho Indians

Retold by
PHILIPPA ALLEN

Drawings by
LOREN HOLMWOOD

COACHWHIP PUBLICATIONS
GREENVILLE, OHIO

Whispering Wind, by Philippa Allen
© 2026 Coachwhip Publications edition

First published 1930
Philippa Allen Reich, c.1905-1986
CoachwhipBooks.com

ISBN 1-61646-627-8
ISBN-13 978-1-61646-627-5

TALES OF THE NAVAHO INDIANS

THE Navahoes were once a great roving nation of Indians. The drama of their thrilling wild life in the past, when they wandered, never at rest, across the deserts and mountains of the Southwest, is echoed in their legends. These were gradually built up to account for the whispering of the wind, the presence of birds, tumble-weeds, bees and other natural phenomena they saw around them in their camps on hills under the open sky.

Neighbors of the Navahoes, but quite different from them, were the Southwestern Indians who dwelt in pueblos, and summer or winter stayed within their homes. Broad House and Blue House were two such pueblos, or Indian villages, in Chaco Canyon in New Mexico. They are in ruins now, but long ago the two were thriving communities.

When the Indian looked about him at the wonders of nature, he gradually formulated ceremonies to express the world as he saw it. The first tale, "The Great Shell of Broad House," is a story of how the bead chant—a nine-days healing ceremony—first became known to the wandering Navahoes. . . .

By special permission the stories in this book are retold from Washington Matthews' *Navaho Legends,* published in 1897 by the American Folklore Society. I have everywhere followed the text of my original in recounting the facts of my legends. But in almost every instance I have striven to simplify the narrative by omitting all statements that lie outside the main trend of the plot, and would thus curb the swift pace of the story.

PHILIPPA ALLEN.

CONTENTS

THE GREAT SHELL OF BROAD HOUSE

THE TREACHERY OF THE PUEBLO PEOPLE

TWO young men, one from Broad House and one from Blue House, went out one day to hunt deer. Wearily returning at sunset, they saw a war-eagle sailing by overhead and stopped to watch his flight. He moved slowly away, growing smaller and smaller until he dwindled to a black speck above the distant horizon.

As the young braves peered after the eagle, it seemed to them that he alighted on the top of Standing Rock, a high cliff of red sandstone in a distant canyon. To mark the spot the boys cut a forked stick and planted it so that, lying on the ground, they could sight through it, the fork guiding their eyes directly to the spot. At dusk the boys went home.

In those days eagles were very scarce in the land. So when the boys reached the villages and told of the adventure, their story created much excitement. All the people desired eagle feathers for their ceremonial robes. They agreed to send four men in the morning to hunt for the eagle's nest.

At dawn the four men found the forked stick and

sighting over it to the top of Standing Rock, they crossed the canyon and climbed the slope in search of the eagle. When the men reached the summit of the rock, they discovered the eagle and its young in a cleft on the face of the precipice below them. All day they watched the nest without being able to reach an eagle feather.

At night they went home and told what they had seen: two young eagles of different ages in the nest. They could be reached only by lowering a man to the nest with a rope. The people took counsel. Who among them would undertake such an adventure? For directly above the nest was an overhanging ledge which anyone descending would be obliged to pass. This made the task dangerous. No one in the pueblos was willing to risk his life.

Now a miserable Navaho beggar lived just outside the villages. He ate any scraps of food he could pick up. When the sweepings of the rooms and the ashes from the fireplaces were thrown out on the kitchen heap, the beggar searched eagerly through them and was happy if he could find a few grains of corn or a piece of paper bread. So the people called him He-Who-Picks-Up.

That evening people of the pueblos invited the poor Navaho to come to the kiva, a large ceremonial chamber. Hospitably they bade him be seated, placed before him a large basket of paper bread, and bowls of boiled corn and meat. They urged him again and again to eat his fill.

"How did that taste to you?" asked his hosts when the Navaho could not take another bite.

"I liked it and I thank you for giving me all this," replied the astonished Navaho.

"You shall eat all your life of such good things," said the people. "Never again will you have to scrape among the dirt for corn if you do as we desire."

Then the men told him of their plan for catching the young eagles by lowering him in a basket to the side of the nest.

"Will you help us, grandchild?" they begged him. The poor man was silent a long time. The people had to ask him four times before he at last answered.

"At best," said the Navaho, "I lead a poor life. Existence is not sweet to a hungry man. It would be pleasant to eat such food for the rest of my days, and some time or other I must die. Therefore I shall do as you wish."

The next morning, just as the sun was coming up, the people awoke the beggar and prepared him a breakfast of mush and venison. While waiting for him to finish his meal, they brought forth a strong carrying-basket. To each of the four corners of the basket a stout cord had been tied. Soon a large party set out from the pueblos for Standing Rock.

When the people had climbed to the top of the

rock, they tied a long rope to the ends of the four cords on the basket.

Then they said to the Navaho, "Here, sit in the basket, and when we let you down opposite the nest, seize the two eaglets and drop them to the bottom of the cliff."

The poor man stepped into the basket which was slowly lowered over the edge of the precipice. As soon as he was on a level with the nest he called to the people above him to stop. But just as the Navaho was about to grasp the eaglets and throw them down Wind whispered to him,

"These people of the Pueblos are not your friends. Do not believe that they will feed you with their good food as long as you live. If you throw these young eagles down, they will never pull you up again. Climb into the nest and stay there."

When he heard this, the Navaho shouted to those above, "Swing the basket nearer to the cliff," and as its rim touched the rock, he scrambled into the nest, leaving an empty basket to rock back and forth in the morning breeze.

The people above waited, expecting to see the Navaho get back into the basket again. But when a time had passed and he did not return they began to call to him as if he were a dear relation of theirs.

"My son," said the old men, "throw down those little eagles."

"My elder brother! My younger brother!" the young men shouted, "throw them down."

They kept up their clamor until nearly sunset, but they did not move the will of the Navaho who sat silently in the cleft. When the sun was low in the west, they left him and went home.

Early next day the people of the villages gathered in a great crowd at the foot of the cliff. They renewed their entreaties, calling the Navaho by endearing names, and displaying all kinds of tempting food to his gaze. All their efforts were in vain—he neither listened nor spoke to them.

On the morning of the third day they came again. This time they came in anger. Instead of friendly names, they sent fire-arrows at the eyrie, hoping to catch the nest on fire so that he would have to throw it down. But he remained watchful and whenever a fire-arrow entered the cleft, he seized it quickly and threw it out. They abused the poor Navaho and reviled him and called him bad names.

When they came on the fourth day, they acted as they had done on the previous day, but they did not succeed in making the Navaho throw down the two young eagles.

He spoke imploringly to the birds, saying, "Can't you help me?"

They rose in the nest, shook their wings, and threw out many little feathers which fell on the people below. The Navaho thought the birds must be scattering disease on his enemies.

The people left saying furiously, "Now we shall leave you to die of hunger and thirst."

THE HOME OF THE EAGLES

WHEN his tormentors were gone he sat in the cave, weak and despairing, till night fell.

Soon after dark he heard a great rushing sound which approached from one side of the cleft, roared a moment in front and then grew faint in the distance at the other side. Four times the sound came and went, growing louder each time it passed, and at length the father Eagle lit on the eyrie. Soon the sounds were repeated and the mother of the eaglets alighted.

Turning at once toward the Navaho, she said, "Greeting, my child! You have not thrown down your younger brothers." The father Eagle repeated the same words. And the Navaho only replied, "I am hungry. I am thirsty."

The father Eagle opened his sash and took out a small white cotton cloth which contained a little corn meal, and a small cup of white shell no bigger than the palm of the hand.

When the Indian saw this he said, "Give me water first, for I am famishing with thirst."

"No," said the Eagle, "eat first and then you shall have something to drink."

Then the Eagle drew forth from among his tail feathers a small plant which had many joints and grows near streams. The joints were filled with water. The Eagle mixed a little of the water with some of the meal in the shell and handed the mixture to the Navaho.

"What a poor meal to offer a man!" thought the Navaho, supposing he would finish it in one mouthful. But he ate and ate and ate and could not empty the cup. When he was satisfied, the shell was as full as it was in the beginning. Then the Eagle put the jointed plant to the Navaho's lips as if it were a wicker bottle, and the Indian drank his fill.

On the previous nights the Navaho had slept between the eagles in the nest to shelter himself from the wind. But on this night the great Eagles slept one on each side of him. Before the Eagles lay down to sleep each took off his robe of plumes which formed a single garment opening in front, and revealed a form like that of a human being.

The Navaho slept well that night and did not waken till he heard a voice calling from the top of the cliff, "Where are you? The day has dawned. It is growing late. Why are you not already abroad?"

At the sound of this voice the Eagles woke, too, and put on their feather robes. Presently a great

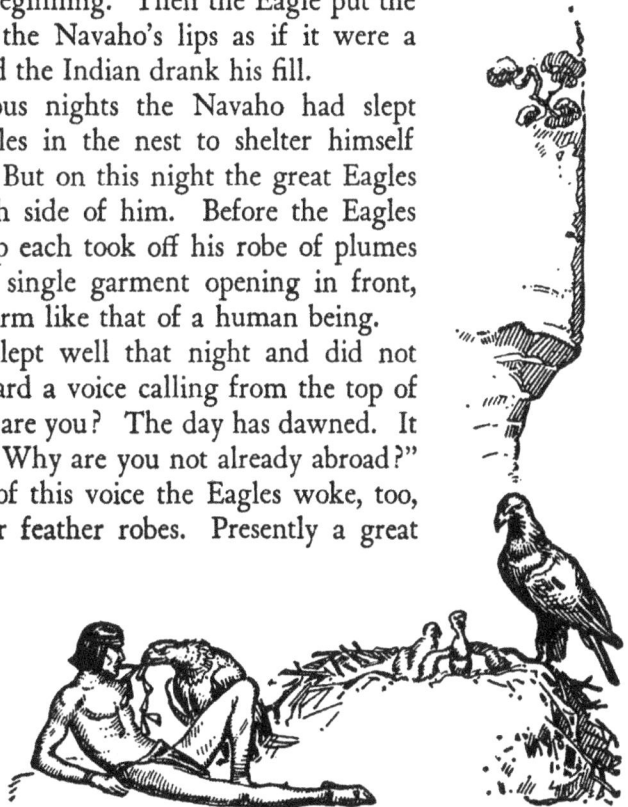

number of birds were seen flying before the cleft and others were heard calling to one another on the rock overhead. There were many kinds of Eagles and Hawks in the throng.

One of the Eagles brought a dress of eagle plumes and was about to put it on the Navaho when the others interfered, and they had a long argument. In the end they all flew away without giving him the feather garment.

On their return they told him they had thought of another plan for moving him from the cleft. They made him lie on his face, while they placed a streak of crooked lightning under his feet, a sunbeam under his outstretched hands, and a rainbow under his forehead. An Eagle then seized each end of these supports and they flew with the Navaho and the eaglets away from the eyrie.

They circled round twice with their burden before they reached the level of the top of the cliff. They circled round twice more ascending, and then flew toward the south, still going upwards. When they got above San Mateo Mountain, they began to flag and breathed hard, and they cried out, "We are weary. We can fly no farther."

The voice of one unseen by the Navaho cried from above, "Let go your burden."

The Eagles released their hold on the supports, and the Navaho felt himself slip and go plunging down.

But he had not fallen far when with a sickening jolt he felt himself seized around his waist and chest. Something was twining itself tightly about his body, and a moment later he beheld the heads of the two Arrow-snakes looking at him over his shoulders. The Arrow-snakes flew with him swiftly upwards through a hole in the sky and landed him safely on the surface of the upper world.

When He-Who-Picks-Up looked around him he saw four villages built like swallows' nests in the hollows of a great canyon. To the east lay a white pueblo of the Wolf Clan, southward a blue pueblo of Blue Fox Clan, in the west a yellow pueblo of Puma Clan, to the north a black pueblo of Big Snake Clan.

The Navaho was left free to go where he chose, but Wind whispered in his ear, "Visit all the pueblos if you wish, except that of the north. Chicken Hawk and other bad characters dwell there."

He entered several of the houses and was well treated wherever he went. In their homes the Eagles were just like ordinary people down on the lower world. As soon as they entered their houses they took off their feather suits, hung them up on pegs, and went around in white suits which they wore underneath their feathers when in flight. He-Who-Picks-Up visited all the pueblos except the black one in the north.

SPIDER WOMAN

IN A few days a war party was organized, and the Navaho determined to go with it. When the warriors started on the trail he followed them.

"Where are you going?" they asked.

"I wish to be one of your party," he replied.

They laughed at him and said, "You are a fool to think you can go to war against such dreadful enemies. We can move as fast as the wind, yet our enemies move faster. If they are able to overcome us, what chance have you, poor man, for your life?"

When he heard this the Navaho remained behind. But the Eagles had not travelled far when he hurried after them. As he came up to them they cried angrily, "What manner of man are you to rush so heedlessly into danger? Go back to the villages."

In the morning when the warriors resumed their march, he remained behind on the camping-ground as if he intended to return; but as soon as they were out of sight he continued to follow them. He had not travelled far when he saw smoke coming up out of the ground. On nearer approach he found a smoke-hole, out of which stuck an old yellow ladder.

The Navaho looked down through the hole and beheld in an underground chamber a strange-looking old woman with a big mouth. Her teeth were not set evenly in her head like those of an Indian. They extended out from her mouth and were curved like the claws of a bear. She was Spider Woman. She invited him into her house, and he climbed down the ladder through the hole in the roof.

When he got inside, the Spider Woman showed him four large wooden hoops—one in the east colored black, one in the south blue, one in the west yellow, and one in the north white and sparkling. Attached to each hoop were a number of decayed, ragged feathers.

"These feathers," she said, "were once beautiful plumes, but now they are old and dirty. I want new plumes to adorn my hoops, and you can get them for me. Many of the Eagles will be killed in the battle to which you are going, and you can pluck out the plumes and bring them to me. Have no fear of the enemies. Do you know who they are? Only bumblebees and tumble-weeds."

She gave him a long black cane and said, "With this wand gather the tumble-weeds into a pile, and then set them on fire. Spit the juice of the scare-weed at the bees and they can not sting you. But before you destroy them, gather some tumble-weed seeds and a few of the nests of the bees. You will need these things when you return to the earth."

Reassured by Spider Woman's words the Navaho went firmly on his way. He soon came up with the

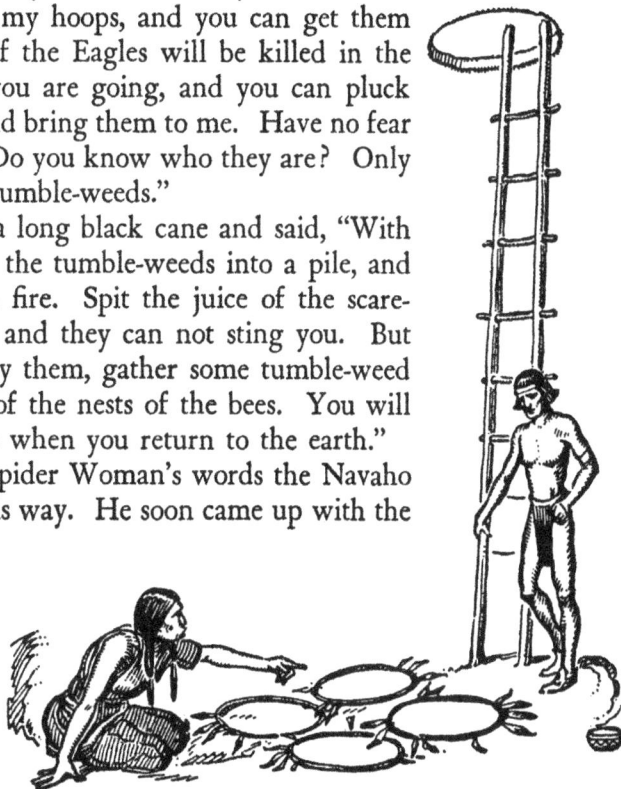

warriors where they were hiding behind a little hill, putting on their war-paint. Some of their number had crept cautiously to the top of the hill to reconnoiter. The Navaho climbed the hill and peered down, but he could see no enemy whatever. Below him was a dry sandy flat, covered here and there with cactus, sunflowers, and dead weeds, for it was now late in the autumn in the world above.

Soon the Eagles were all ready for the fray. They raised their war-cry and charged down the hill into the sandy plain. As the Navaho stared after them, furnace blasts of breeze lifted the sand in his face and he knew a great wind was rising.

When the warriors approached the plain, a small whirlwind glided towards them, picking up a great number of tumble-weeds which surged madly around through the air as the dust-spout whirled higher and higher. At the same time with a sibilant warning a cloud of bumblebees arose from a patch of sunflowers.

The Eagles charged through the ranks of the bees and then turned around and charged back again. Some spread their wings and soared aloft to attack the tumble-weeds that had gone up with the whirlwind. From time to time the Navaho noticed the dark body of an Eagle falling down through the air.

The fighting had gone on some time, when the Navaho saw a few of the Eagles turn and run toward

The Eagles charged through the ranks of the bees and
then turned and charged back again

the hill where he lay watching. In a moment the
whole party of Eagles deserted the field and rushed
past him in disorderly retreat, leaving the slain
behind. Soon the wind fell, the tumble-weeds lay
quiet again on the sand, and the bumblebees disappeared among the sunflowers.

Then He-Who-Picks-Up walked boldly down to
the sandy flat. He raked the tumble-weeds together,
and, after he had tied some of the seeds into a corner
of his shirt, set the weeds on fire with his drill. Re-
membering Spider Woman's advice, he gathered
some scare-weed before he went in among the
sunflowers. The bees collected around him in a great
swarm and tried to sting him, but he spat the juice
of the scare-weed at them and killed all that he
struck. The rest fled in fear.

With his black wand the Navaho dug into the
ground and got some of their nests and honey; he
took a couple of young bees and tied their feet
together—and all these things he put into the corner
of his blanket.

With the bees out of the way the Navaho thought
of the wishes of his friend, Spider Woman. He went
around among the dead eagles plucking as many
plumes as he could grasp in both hands.

Spider Woman was delighted with these feathers
when he delivered them. "Thank you, grandchild,"
she said, "you have brought me the plumes I have

long wanted, and you have done a great service to your friends, the Eagles, by slaying their enemies."

He slept that night on the trail and next morning reached the canyon of the eagles. As he toiled up the steep slope to the village of the Fox Clan he heard from afar the cries of mourners.

When he entered the pueblo walls, people crowded around him and said, "Those who returned told us you had been killed in the fight, and we have been mourning for you."

The Navaho made no reply, but took from his blanket the two young bumblebees and swung them around his head. All the people were terrified and ran, and they did not stop running till they got safely behind their houses.

In a little while their courage returned and they came slowly back to him. Then He-Who-Picks-Up laid the two bees on the ground, took out the seeds of the tumble-weeds and laid them beside the bees, and said to the Eagle People, "My friends, here are the children of your enemies. And seeing these you may know that I have slain the rest of them."

There was great rejoicing among the people when they heard this. The principal men from all the pueblos came to thank him.

The next morning the Navaho went over to the sky-hole, taking with him the young bees and the seeds of the tumble-weeds. To them he said, "Go down to the land of the Navahoes and multiply there. But if you ever cause them sorrow and trouble, as you have caused the people of this land, I shall destroy you again." As he spoke he flung them down to earth.

THE TRIUMPH OF THE POOR NAVAHO

THE Navaho remained in the towns of the Eagle People twenty-four days, during which he was taught their songs, prayers and ceremonies. Then the Eagles told him it was time for him to return to the earth. They put a robe of eagle plumage on him and led him to the sky-hole.

They said, "When you came up from the lower world you were heavy and had to be carried by others. Henceforth you will be light and can move through the air with your own power."

He spread his wings. The Eagles blew a powerful breath behind him, and he drifted down to the summit of San Mateo Mountain.

He-Who-Picks-Up went to his own relations among the Navahoes. But the odors of their hogan, a little house built low against the yellow face of the desert, were intolerable to him. He left it and sat outside in the blistering sun. Then his relatives built him a medicine-lodge where he might sit by himself. They bathed his younger brother, dressed

him in new raiment and sent him to learn what his elder brother could tell him. The brothers spent twelve days in the lodge together, while the older instructed the younger in all the rites and songs of the Eagles.

After this the Navaho went to visit the people of Broad House, who had been so treacherous, but they did not recognize him, now that he was sleek and well fed and beautifully dressed in a fine buckskin shirt and embroidered moccasins. They had long since ceased to think of the poor beggar whom they had left to die in the eagles' nest.

He-Who-Picks-Up noticed that there were many sore and lame in the village. A new disease, they told him, had broken out among them. This was the disease which they had caught from the feathers of the eaglets when they were attacking the nest.

"I have a brother," said the Navaho, "who is a powerful medicine-man. He knows a rite that will cure this disease."

The people of the village consulted together and decided to employ his brother to perform the ceremony over their sick ones.

"To perform the rite properly," said the Navaho, "I must be the first dancer. Bring me strings of your finest shell beads to wear on my legs and forearms and strings of your best turquoise to wear around my neck. I must have so many of them that I will not be able to bend my head. Then find me the largest shell basins in Broad House and Blue House—the largest to hang on my back and the next size to hang on my chest."

Wind told him that the greatest shell basin the pueblos had was so large that if he tried to embrace it around the edge, his finger-tips would scarcely meet, and that this shell he must insist on having. The next largest shell, Wind assured him, was but little smaller.

They brought him some great shell basins which they said were the ones he wanted. But he measured them with his arms, and finding that his hands joined easily, he discarded them. They brought him larger and larger shells, and tried to persuade him to use them, but he rejected them all with contempt.

On the day of the dance they brought him with reluctance the great shell of Broad House and the great shell of Blue House. He clasped the first in his arms and his fingers did not meet on the opposite side. When he clasped the second, the tips of his fingers just met.

"These," said he proudly, "are the shells I must wear when I dance."

In the evening the village people built a great circle of branches. They lighted the fires and dressed He-Who-Picks-Up in all their fine beads and shells just as he had asked. They put the great shell of Broad

House on his back and the great shell of Blue House on his chest, and another shell on his forehead. Then the Navaho began to dance to soft drum-taps, and his brother, the medicine-man, to sing a chant of such wild beauty that all were deeply moved.

The song was strange to the village people and they all wondered what it could mean. But they soon found out when they saw that the dancing Navaho was rising slowly from the ground. He-Who-Picks-Up was rising toward the sky with the great shell of Broad House and all the wealth of the pueblos in shell-beads and turquoise jewelry on his swarthy body.

They screamed wildly to him and called him by all sorts of dear names—father, brother, son—to come down again, but the more they called the higher he rose. When his feet had risen above them they observed that a streak of white lightning which passed under his feet like a rope, was hanging from a dark cloud that gathered above. It was the gods who were lifting him, for the legends say it is thus that gods lift mortals to the sky.

When the village people found that no persuasion could induce the Navaho to return, some called for ropes that they might seize him and pull him down. But he was soon beyond the reach of their longest rope. Then a shout was raised for arrows that they might shoot him. But before the arrows could be

found he was lost to sight in the black cloud and was never more seen on earth.

The Pueblo People bewailed their loss. But ever after at Standing Rock the Navahoes practised the rite of the bead chant, or nine-day healing ceremony, of their early ancestor.

THE LOSS OF A GREAT GAMBLER

THE way Broad House came to be built was this:
Long ago a gambling god named Nohoilpi,
He-Who-Wins-Men, came to live in the neighborhood of the Pueblo People in Chaco Canyon.
Nohoilpi had for a lucky piece a large turquoise
stone, and when he challenged the people to games
and contests, he won from them repeatedly. The
Pueblos lost their property, their women and children, and finally some of the men themselves. Then
the gambler Nohoilpi told them he would give them
part of their property back in payment if they would
build him a great house.

When the Navahoes wandered from their lonely
hidden camps into Chaco Canyon, they found the
Pueblo People busy building a rectangular stone
house at the base of a great cliff. The first story had
many small rooms, the outer rooms for dwellings
and the inner for granaries, and one large central
ceremonial chamber. On one side of the house
workmen were beginning on the second story apartments set well back from the walls of the first story.
So impressed were the Navahoes with this pyramidal

structure that they named it Broad House. In the plaza, a level space in front of the house, some of the women were making a race-track and preparing for games of chance.

When all was in readiness for the games, four days' notice was given. And messengers sent to the neighboring canyon stronghold of Blue House came back with twelve men to compete with He-Who-Wins-Men. The men of Blue House staked their liberty and after a brief contest they lost themselves to the great gambler.

Again a notice of four days was given, and again twelve men of Blue House came to play. These, too, lost their liberty. The third time an announcement was given women were among the contestants, but they were no more successful than the men had been. All were put to work building Broad House for their new master.

When the children of Blue House came to win back their parents, they only succeeded in adding themselves to the number of the gambler's slaves. Soon all the people of Blue House had lost their freedom, among them the chief of the pueblo.

Up to this time the Navahoes had kept count of the winnings of Nohoilpi, but now people from other pueblos came in such numbers to play and lose that they could keep track no longer. These new victims, in addition to staking their freedom, gambled away beads, shells, turquoises and all their wealth. It was not long with the labor of so many slaves until the great Broad House was finished.

All this time the Navahoes had been merely spectators and had taken no part in the games. One day the voice of Talking God was heard faintly in the distance crying, "Wu' hu' hu' hu." His voice sounded, as it always does, four times, each time nearer. Immediately after the last call, which was loud and clear, Talking God appeared at the door of a hut of a young childless Navaho couple.

He made signs to the young man over the curtain which hung in the doorway, bidding him come out. The god signaled the Navaho that the people of Blue House had lost two enormous shells to Nohoilpi, which were their chief treasures. The Sun Father, he said, had coveted these shells and had begged the gambler for them; but Nohoilpi had refused and the Sun was angry.

As a result of all this, said Talking God, certain divine ones were to meet in the mountains in twelve days to hold council. He invited the young man to be present at the meeting and disappeared.

The Navaho counted the passing days and on the twelfth said to his wife, "I go now to the council of the divine ones, but I shall come back as soon as I can and tell you all that I have heard."

"It is well," she replied. So the young man set

out to the southwest, on the trail to the secret laby-
rinth of Thunder Mountain.

After a steep climb the Navaho reached the council
chamber. There were Talking God, House God and
his son, Young House God. Wind, Darkness, Bat,
and Great Snake also were there, and Little Bird,
Gopher, and many others. The young Navaho was
surprised to observe that a number of the gambler's
domesticated animals were also present. They were
anxious to be free, so Wind had spoken to them and
they had entered into the plot against Nohoilpi.

All night the gods danced and sang and performed
their mystic rites around the son of House God.
This was to give him powers as a gambler equal to
those of He-Who-Wins-Men. When morning came
they dressed the young god in clothes exactly like
those of the gambler and molded his form and face
to look as much like the gambler as possible. Then
they consulted as to what other means they should
take to outwit Nohoilpi.

One of the games they proposed to play was called
Thirteen Chips. It was played with thirteen thin
flat pieces of wood which were colored red on one
side and white on the other side. The winner was
the one who had the greatest number of chips fall
white side up after they had been thrown in the air.

"Leave the game to me," said the Bat. "I have
made thirteen chips that are white on both sides. I

will hide myself in the ceiling, and when our champion throws up his chips I will catch them and drop down my chips instead."

Another game was Push on the Wood. In this the contestants push against a tree until it is torn from its roots and falls.

"I will see that this game is won," said Gopher. "I will gnaw the roots of the tree, so that he who shoves it may easily make it fall."

In the game of Ball, the object was to hit the ball so that it would fall beyond a certain line.

"I will win this game for you," said Little Bird, "for I will hide within the ball and fly with it wherever I want to go. Do not hit the ball hard. Give it only a light tap and depend on me to carry it."

The gambler's pets begged Wind to blow hard, so that they might have an excuse to give their master for not keeping due watch when he was in danger. In the morning the Wind blew for them a strong gale. The whole party of conspirators left the mountain at dawn and came down to the brow of the canyon above Broad House to wait there until sunrise.

Nohoilpi had two wives, who were the prettiest women in the whole land. Wherever either of them went, she carried a stick in her hands with something tied on the end of it, as a sign that she was the wife of the great gambler.

On the brow of a cliff at sunrise the watchers saw
one of the wives coming out of the gambler's house
with a water-jar on her head. Thereupon the son
of House God descended into the canyon and
followed her to the spring. She was not aware of his
presence until she had filled her water-jar, and then
she supposed it to be her own husband. But as he
approached nearer, the woman soon discovered her
error. However, she deemed it prudent to say
nothing, and quietly permitted him to follow her
into Broad House.

As he pushed aside the robe which hung at the
entrance of the ceremonial chamber, the young son
of House God saw that many of the slaves had already assembled within. Perhaps they were aware
that some trouble was in store for their master.

Nohoilpi felt jealous when he saw the stranger
entering after his wife. He looked up with an angry
face, asking at once, "Have you come to gamble with
me?" This he repeated four times, and each time
the young god said, "No."

"The stranger fears to play with me," thought
Nohoilpi. So he went on challenging the son of
House God recklessly, "I'll bet my legs against your
legs," he said, "my arms against your arms, and my
hair against your hair." Nor did He-Who-Wins-
Men stop until he had bet every part of his body
against the same part of his adversary.

In the meantime the party of gods, who had been watching from above, descended to Broad House, and people from the neighboring pueblos arrived, among them two boys who were dressed in women's clothes like those of Nohoilpi's wives.

Young House God pointed to them and said, "I will bet my wives against your wives."

Nohoilpi accepted the wager, and the four, two women and two mock-women, were led aside to sit in a row near the wall.

First He-Who-Wins-Men challenged the stranger to a game of Thirteen Chips. With Bat assisting from the rafters as he had promised, the son of House God won the game, and with it the wives of the disappointed gambler.

Then they went out into the plaza to play the other games. First they tried nanzoz. The track already prepared lay east and west, but, prompted by Wind, the stranger insisted on having a track made from north to south, and, again at the bidding of Wind, he chose the red stick. Young House God threw the hoop and at first it seemed about to fall on the gambler's pole, but to the great surprise of Nohoilpi it rolled farther on and fell on the pole of his opponent. Young House God ran to pick up the hoop, lest Nohoilpi in doing so might hurt the snake inside, but the gambler was so angry that he threw his stick away and gave up the game. He hoped to do better in the next contest, which was that of pushing down pinyon trees.

For this He-Who-Wins-Men pointed out two small trees, but the son of House God insisted that larger trees must be found. After some searching, they agreed upon two of good size which grew close together, and Wind whispered to the youth which one he must select. The gambler strained with all his might at his tree, but could not move it, but when his opponent's turn came, the stranger shoved the other tree over with little effort, for all its roots had been severed by Gopher.

Then followed a variety of games, on which Nohoilpi staked his wealth in shells and precious stones, his houses, and many of his slaves. Steadily he lost them all.

The last game was that of Ball. On the line over which the ball was to be knocked all the people were assembled. On one side stood the Pueblo Indians who still remained slaves. On the other side were the freedmen and all those who had come to wager themselves, in a last desperate attempt to rescue their enslaved kinsmen.

Nohoilpi bet the last of his slaves on this game and even his own person. He struck his ball a heavy blow, but it did not reach the line. The stranger gave his but a light tap, and the bird within flew with it far beyond the line. With a shout the re-

*With the labor of so many slaves it was not long until
the great Broad House was finished*

leased captives jumped over the line and joined their overjoyed people.

The victor ordered that all the shells, beads, and precious stones, and the two great shells be brought forth. He gave the beads and shells to Talking God that they might be distributed among the gods. The two great shells were given to the Sun.

In the meantime Nohoilpi sat to one side saying bitter things, bemoaning his fate, and cursing and threatening his enemies. "I will kill you all with the lightning. I will send war and disease among you. May the cold freeze you! May the fire burn you! May the waters drown you!" he cried.

"He had cursed enough," whispered Wind in the ear of Young House God. "Put an end to his angry words."

The young victor called Nohoilpi to him and said, "You have bet yourself and have lost. You are now my slave and must do my bidding. You are not a god, for my power has prevailed against yours."

The son of House God had a magic bow named the Bow of Darkness. He bent this upwards, and placing the string on the ground he bade his slave stand on the string. Then he shot Nohoilpi up into the sky as if he had been an arrow. Up and up he went, growing smaller and smaller to the sight till he faded to a mere speck and finally disappeared altogether. As He-Who-Wins-Men flew upwards he was heard to mutter in angry tones, but no one could distinguish anything he said as he ascended.

Nohoilpi flew up in the sky until he came to the home of Moon-Bearer, the god who carries the moon. Very old he is and dwells in a long row of stone houses. When Nohoilpi arrived there, he related his brutal misfortune in the lower world. "Now I am poor," he said, "and this is why I have come to see you."

"You need be poor no longer," said kindly Moon-Bearer. "I will provide for you."

He made for the gambler domestic animals of a different kind from those he had had in Chaco valley —sheep, asses, horses, swine, goats and fowls. He gave him cloths of bright colors, more beautiful than those woven by his slaves at Broad House. Then, too, he made a new people, the Mexicans, for the gambler to rule over. And when Moon-Bearer sent Nohoilpi forth into the world again, the gambler descended far to the south of his former home and reached the earth in old Mexico.

Nohoilpi's people increased greatly in Mexico, and after a while they began to move towards the north, and build towns along the Rio Grande. Nohoilpi came with them until they arrived at a place north of Santa Fe. There they ceased building, and he returned to old Mexico, where the gambler still lives, and where he is now the god of the Mexicans.

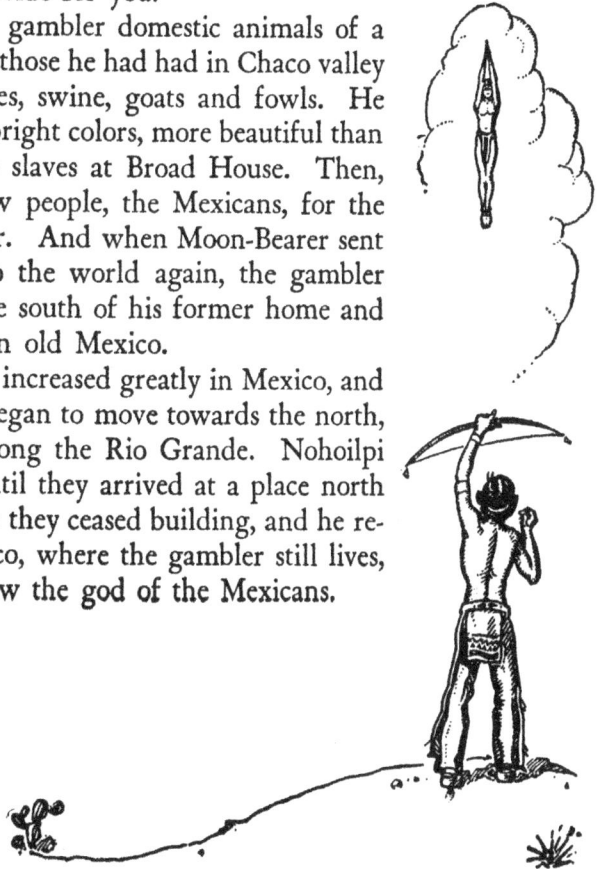

The Navaho who went at the bidding of Talking
God to the tryst of gods stayed with them till the
gambler was shot into the sky. Then he returned
to his people and told them all he had seen.

THE TRAIL OF TWO YOUNG WARRIORS

GODS TO LOVE AND GODS TO FEAR

TWO sons were born to the sisters, White-Shell-Woman and Woman-Who-Changes. The gods, Water Sprinkler and Talking God, were glad and made for the children two baby baskets, both alike. The foot rests and the backs they made of sunbeam, the hoods of rainbow, the side-strings of sheet lightning, and the lacing strings of zigzag lightning. They covered one child with a black cloud, and the other with a blanket of distant rain. Calling the children Sinali, or Grandchildren, they went away, promising to return to see them at the end of four days.

When the gods came back, the babies had grown to be the size of boys twelve years old. And the gods said to them, "Boys, we have come to have a race with you." They chose a footpath that went around a neighboring mountain and started out—two boys and two gods.

Before the long race was half finished the boys, who had run fast, began to pant and stumble on the rough slopes. And the gods, who were still fresh, got behind them and beat them with twigs of moun-

41

tain mahogany. Talking God won the race, and
the boys came home rubbing their sore backs. Then
the gods departed, saying "We will be back in another four days."

As soon as they were gone Wind whispered to the
lads, "Those old ones are not such fleet runners. If
you would get out and practice for the next four days,
you might win after all."

So for four days the boys ran hard many times a
day around the mountain and when the gods came
back again the youths had grown tall and strong.

Now in the second race the gods began to gasp
for breath, and then the boys with delight drew up
behind their elders and whipped them to increase
their speed. The oldest boy won and this pleased
the gods so that they laughed and clapped their
hands, for they admired the spirit and prowess of
the young braves.

That night, after the race the boys lay down on
their bed of skins as usual. Their mothers were
whispering together in a corner and they lay un-
moving to listen. But, as much as they strained
their ears, they could not hear a word.

At length they rose, approached the women and
asked, "Mothers, what are you talking about?"

And the women answered, "It is nothing."

"Grandmothers," implored the boys, "do tell us
what you were saying."

"No," replied the mothers shaking their heads, "it was nothing."

"Then tell us who our fathers are," demanded the boys sullenly.

And the women replied, "The round cactus and the sitting cactus are your fathers."

Next day the sisters made rude bows of juniper wood, and arrows.

These they gave to the boys and said, "Go and play, but do not go out of sight of the hogan, and do not go to the west."

In spite of this warning the boys stole off unnoticed by the anxious women, who would keep them at home, and walked a long way to the west. A great dark bird with a red skinny head that had no feathers on it was the only living thing they saw. They drew their arrows and pointed them at the bird, but before they could shoot, the bird spread its wings and flew a long way off.

When they reached home they said, "Mothers, we have been to the west, and we have seen a great dark bird whose head was red and bare. We tried to shoot it, but it flew away before we could discharge our arrows."

"Alas!" said the women, "It was Dzeso, the Buzzard. He is the spy for the enemy god, who kicks men down cliffs."

The following day, although again strictly warned

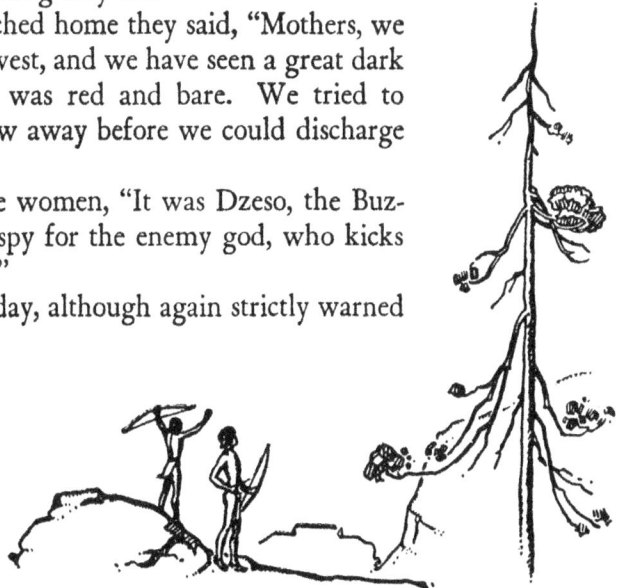

not to go far from the house, the boys wandered far
to the north. Across a sharp-walled canyon they
saw a bird of black plumage perched on a tree. It
was talking to itself, saying "a'a'i'." They aimed at
it, but it spread its wings and tail and disappeared
down the canyon. As it flew, the boys noticed that
its plumes were edged with white. When they got
home they told their mothers what they had seen.

"That bird," said the women, "is the Magpie. He
is the spy for the gods, who slay people with their
eyes. Alas, our children! What shall we do to save
you? You would not listen to us. Now the spies
of the alien gods have seen you. They will tell their
chiefs, and soon the monsters will come here to
devour you, as they have all boys before you."

Next morning the sisters made a corncake and laid
it on the ashes to bake. White-Shell-Woman went
out of the hogan, and as she did so she saw Yeitso,
the tallest and fiercest of the alien gods approaching.
She ran quickly back inside and gave warning, and
Woman-Who-Changes hid the boys under a pile of
sticks in the corner.

Yeitso came and sat down at the door, just as the
women were taking the cake from the baking oven.

"That cake is for me," growled the giant Yeitso,
"how nice it smells."

"No," said Woman-Who-Changes sharply, "it was
not meant for your great maw."

"I don't care," retorted Yeitso. "I would rather eat boys. Where are your boys? I have come to make a meal of them."

"We have none," said Woman-Who-Changes. "All the boys were killed by your people long ago."

"No boys?" exclaimed the giant. "Then what made all these tracks around here?"

"Oh! those are some I made for fun," replied the woman. "I am lonely here, and I make them to pretend there are many people around me."

She showed Yeitso how she could make tracks with her fist. He compared the two sets of tracks, seemed to be satisfied, and went away.

When he was gone, White-Shell-Woman went up to the top of a neighboring hill to look around. She saw many of the enemy gods hastening in their direction, and ran speedily back to tell her sister. Woman-Who-Changes took four colored hoops and threw a white one to the east, a blue one to the south, a yellow one to the west, and a black one to the north. Instantly a great gale arose, blowing so fiercely from the hogan that none of the enemies could make headway against it.

THE BOYS SEEK THEIR FATHER

NEXT morning the boys got up before daybreak and stole away. The women missed
them, but could not trace them in the dark. When
it was light enough to examine the ground the sisters
went out to look for fresh tracks. They found four
footprints of each boy, pointing in the direction of
Encircled Mountain. More than these they could
not discover, so they came to the conclusion that the
boys had taken the rainbow trail, a holy path, and
gave up further search.

The boys traveled rapidly on the rainbow trail.
Near Encircled Mountain, soon after sunrise, they
saw smoke arising from the ground. A ladder,
black with smoke, projected from a hole in the roof
of an underground chamber.

Looking down onto the chamber they saw Spider
Woman, who glanced up at them and said:

"Hello, children. Come on down and let me see
you. Who are you? Where do you come from?"

The lads made no answer but ran rapidly down
the ladder. When they reached the floor she asked
them again, "Where are you two going together?"

"Nowhere in particular," they answered, "we came
here because we had no place else to go."

"Would you like to find your father?" she asked.

"Yes," they answered, "but we do not know the way to his hogan."

"Ah!" said the woman, "it is a long and dangerous way to the house of the Sun. There are many enemy gods living between here and your father's house. But I shall give you something to subdue your enemies and keep you alive."

She gave the lads for a charm to preserve their lives, a hoop with two life-feathers (feathers plucked from a living eagle) attached. And they thanked her and started eagerly on their way.

Soon they saw Rocks-That-Crush looming up ahead of them. These were two high cliffs on either side of a narrow chasm through which the trail led. When the boys came to the chasm, they lifted their feet as if to enter and the rocks opened to let them in. Then the boys put down their feet, but withdrew them quickly. The rocks closed with a snap, like hands clapping, to crush them, but the boys were safely outside. Four times did they deceive the rocks in this way.

Then the rocks cried out (for they were really people and thought like men), "Who are you, where do you come from and where are you going?"

"We are children of the Sun," answered the boys. "We come from Encircled Mountain, and we go to seek the house of our father." They repeated the words of a chant Spider Woman had taught them.

Subdued, the rocks said, "Pass on." And they went
safely through the chasm.

Late in the afternoon the boys came to a great plain
covered with cane cactuses. They were looking
around for a way to cross the field, when the ranks
of the cactuses opened, showing a clear passage
through to the other side. The boys pretended to
enter, but retreated. As they did so the ranks closed
together as swiftly as the rocks had done. These
cactuses, like evil spirits, rushed at and tore to pieces
whoever attempted to pass through them. But the
boys tamed them as easily as they had done Rocks-
That-Crush, and passed on in safety.

AT THE HOUSE OF THE SUN

THE house of the Sun God shone in a blue
haze across the plain. Built of turquoise, it was
square and many-storied like a pueblo and stood on
the shore of a great water.

As the boys approached they found the way
guarded by two bears who crouched one to the right
and one to the left, their noses pointing in. Growl-
ing angrily the bears rose as if to attack the children,
but the older boy hastily chanted the magic words of
Spider Woman. When he came to the last words,
"Be still," the bears sank down on their haunches,
completely silenced.

The boys walked on into the shining pueblo. As they entered the ceremonial chamber they saw two handsome young men, Black Thunder and Blue Thunder, seated in the south. In the north were two beautiful maidens.

The maidens glanced at the strangers and then looked down. But the young men gazed at them more closely. The boys explained, "We are seeking our father, the Sun."

Black Thunder and Blue Thunder rose without speaking. They took the four coverings of the sky, wrapped the boys up in them, and stowed them away on a shelf.

A rattle over the door began to shake and one of the young girls said, "Our father is coming."

When Tsohanoai, Bearer-of-the-Sun, entered he took the sun off his back and hung it carelessly on a peg on the west wall, where it shook, clanging "tla, tla, tla, tla." Then he turned to his daughters and said, in an angry tone, "Who were those two I saw come in this door?"

The girls answered, "Two young men seeking their father," and pointed to the bundle on the shelf.

Tsohanoai took down the bundle and unrolled the robe of dawn with which it was covered, then the robe of blue sky, next the robe of yellow evening light, and lastly the robe of darkness. When he unrolled this the boys fell out on the floor. Tsohanoai looked at them and said, "I wish it were indeed true that they were my children."

To his older sons, those who lived with him, he said, "Go out and prepare the sweat-house. Heat for it four of the hardest boulders you can find."

Niltsi, Wind, heard this and thought, "He seeks to kill his children. How shall I avert the danger?"

The sweat-house was built against a bank. Crawling inside, Niltsi dug a hole into the bank and concealed the opening with a flat stone. Then he whispered the secret of the hole into the ears of the boys and said, "Do not hide in the hole until you have answered the questions of your father." The boys went into the sweat-house. Great hot boulders were put in and the opening covered with four sky blankets.

Tsohanoai called, "Are you hot?"

And they answered, "Yes, very hot."

Then they crept into the hiding-place and lay there. After a while Tsohanoai came and poured water through the top of the sweat-house on the stones, and with a loud noise the stones burst. When the stones had cooled somewhat, the boys crept out of their hiding-place. Bearer-of-the-Sun came and asked again, "Are you hot?" thinking he would get no reply. But the boys still answered patiently, "Yes, very hot."

Then their father took the coverings off the sweat-house and let them come out. Satisfied now that the boys were his children, he greeted them in a friendly way. He bade them enter his house.

The four sky blankets were spread on the ground one over another, for the youths to recline on. Tsohanoai held his pipe up to the sun on the wall to light it. When it was drawing satisfactorily, he took the pipe from his mouth and said, "Now, my children, what do you want from me? Why did you come here?"

"Oh, father!" they replied, "the land where we dwell is filled with enemy gods, who devour the people. A giant, Yeitso, is the fiercest of them all. He has eaten nearly all of our kind; there are few left. We had to run away ourselves to escape this terrible Yeitso. Give us, we beg, weapons with which to slay him."

"I will give you weapons for war," agreed Tsohanoai, "and I shall hurl the first bolt at him, myself."

He put into their hands a chain-lightning arrow, a sheet-lightning arrow, a sunbeam arrow, a rainbow arrow, and a great stone knife. From pegs around the room he lifted down armor for each boy.

"These are what we want," said the boys, as they put on the metal clothes and streaks of lightning shot from every joint.

THE BATTLE WITH THE GIANT

NEXT morning Tsohanoai led the boys out to the edge of the world where the sky and the earth came close together, and beyond which there was no world. Then Bearer-of-the-Sun put on his robe of cloud and taking one of his sons under each arm, rose into the heavens.

They journeyed till they came to the hole in the center of the sky. The hole is edged with four smooth, shining cliffs that slope steeply downwards. On the smooth slopes the Sun seated the children and they shot down to the broad top of Tsotsil, San Mateo Mountain.

The two boys descended the mountain on its south side and walked toward Warm Spring. As they passed under a high bluff, they heard voices hailing them, "Hello! where are you going?"

Looking up they saw in the mouth of a cavern above, four holy people—Holy Man, Holy Young Man, Holy Boy, and Holy Girl.

The brothers stayed all night with these people who could tell them all they wanted to know about Yeitso. They said, "We have seen him. He comes down every day from Tsotsil to Warm Spring to drink. When he stoops to the water, one hand rests on Tsotsil and the other on the high hills on the opposite side of the valley, while his feet stretch as far as a man could walk between sunrise and noon."

At daybreak the young braves left the cave and trudged on to Warm Spring. When they came to the edge of the lake, one brother said to the other, "Let us try one of our father's weapons."

They shot one of the lightning arrows at Tsotsil. It made a great cleft in the mountain, which remains to this day, and one said to the other, "We cannot be defeated with such weapons as these."

Soon after, they heard thunderous footsteps, and saw the head of Yeitso peering over a high hill in the east. In a moment the monster raised his head and chest over a hill in the south. Then he appeared as far as his waist over a hill in the west and when he reached Tsotsil in the north he descended the mountain and came to the edge of the lake.

Four times Yeitso bent to the lake to drink, and each time the water lowered perceptibly. When he was through, the lake was nearly drained.

The brothers lost their presence of mind at sight of the giant, and remained motionless while he was stooping down. But as he took his last drink they strode to the edge of the lake and Yeitso saw their reflection in the water.

He raised his head and roared, "What a pretty pair have come in sight! Where have I been hunting that I never saw them before?"

"Throw his words back in his mouth," said the younger to the older brother.

"What a great thing has come in sight! Where have we been hunting?" shouted the older brother.

These taunts were repeated four times by each party. Then the brothers heard Wind whisper quickly, "Ako'! Ako'! Beware! Beware!"

They were standing on a bent rainbow. When they heard the warning, they straightened out the rainbow and descended to the ground. At the same instant a lightning bolt, hurled by Yeitso, passed thundering over their heads.

He hurled four bolts rapidly. As he hurled the second, they bent their rainbow and rose, while the bolt passed under their feet. As he discharged the third they shot down and the lightning passed over them. When he threw the fourth bolt they bent the rainbow very high, for this time he aimed higher. But his weapon still passed under their feet.

Yeitso drew a fifth bolt to throw at them. At this moment Bearer-of-the-Sun threw a bolt from the sky at the head of the giant and he reeled beneath it. Then the older brother sped a chain-lightning arrow and his enemy tottered toward the east. The second arrow made him stumble toward the south. At the third lightning arrow he toppled toward the west, and at the fourth to the north. Then he fell flat on his face and moved no more.

Then the brothers approached their fallen enemy. The younger one scalped him. Up to this time the younger brother had been called Child-of-the-Water. Now his brother gave him the warrior name, He-Who-Cuts-Around. And the older brother himself was called ever after, Slayer-of-Alien-Gods.

The young warriors put the broken arrows of Yeitso and his scalp into a basket and set out for their home. When they reached their mother's hogan, they took off their suits of armor and hid them with the basket in the bushes.

The mothers, who had feared their sons were lost, rejoiced to see them. They asked, "Where have you been since you left here yesterday?"

Slayer-of-Alien-Gods replied, "We have been to the house of our father, the Sun. We have been to Tsotsil and we have slain Yeitso."

"Ah, my child," said Woman-Who-Changes, "do not speak thus. It is wrong to make fun of such an awful monster."

"Do you not believe me?" said Slayer-of-Alien-Gods, "come out, then, and see what we have brought."

He led the women to the hidden basket and showed them the trophies of Yeitso. When they saw them they were convinced and rejoiced. That night they danced to celebrate the victory.

THE FARM AT END-OF-THE-WATER

NEAR Encircled Mountain lived the Navaho, Natinesthani, He-Who-Teaches-Himself. He loved to gamble but was not successful. He lost not only all his own goods, but those of his family as well.

At last one day nothing was left and the mind of Natinesthani was filled with sad thoughts. "My brother disowns me," he said to himself. "My parents refuse me shelter. My niece, whom I love most, barely looks at me. I shall go away and never come back."

As he wandered sadly by the San Juan River and stood gazing at the swift current from a clump of cottonwood trees on the bank, an idea came to him. From the trunk of a tree he would make a hollow vessel in which he could float down the river.

He found a tree that suited him. Plastering mud around the trunk to keep the fire from destroying the whole tree, he burned it off squarely at the base. It took him four days to burn a hole in the top of the log, long enough and wide enough to hold his body comfortably.

When this was finished, the Navaho returned to his grandmother's to say good-by. His niece cooked several wood-rats and ground for him a good quantity of the seeds of wild plants that she had gathered. These provisions she put in a bag of wood-rat skins sewed together, and gave to Natinesthani.

As the Navaho left the hogan to return to the log, his glance fell upon his niece's pet turkey that roosted on a tree nearby. And at the same time Wind whispered in his ear, "Take the turkey along."

"My niece," said Natinesthani turning back, "Wind bids me take your turkey, and I would gladly do so, for I am going among strange people. The bird would be company and remind me of my home. Yet I shall not take him against your will."

"You may have him," she generously replied. And Natinesthani left with the turkey under his arm.

While the Navaho was busy dragging his heavy log canoe down to the water, the gods gathered in council. They decided to help He-Who-Teaches-Himself by preparing his pet turkey for the journey. Unknown to the Indian, they put corn and beans of all colors, and squash, watermelon, muskmelon, and gourd seed under the bird's wings.

Then Natinesthani climbed into the canoe with the bird, and the gods covered the log with black mist and black cloud. Some of the gods who stood on the banks pushed the log with their plumed

wands, until it got into a straight course with its
head pointed down stream.

The log floated steadily with the current. All
went well till it approached the end of San Juan
River. There, surrounded by mountains, is a large
whirling lake called End-of-the-Water. When the
log entered the lake it whirled dizzily around and
around the edge. At last it caught on a rock on the
south shore and the Navaho and the turkey got out
on firm ground.

They walked down a small winding valley till
they came to a beautiful flat, through which ran a
stream. "This would be a good place for a farm,"
thought the Navaho.

The man sat down and the turkey gamboled
around him. "My pet," said the Navaho with long-
ing, "what a beautiful farm I could make here if I
only had the seeds."

When the turkey heard this, it ran a little way to
the east and shook its wings, from which four grains
of white corn dropped out. It ran to the south and
four grains of blue corn fell down. To the west it
scattered four grains of yellow corn, to the north
grains of mixed colors. As it ran back to its astonished master and shook its wings, pumpkin seeds,
watermelon seeds, muskmelon seeds, and beans
rained down.

"E'yehe!" breathed the Indian delightedly, "I see

the gods gave you something for me.   Many thanks, my dear pet."

Natinesthani set to work.   He cut two planting sticks, one of greasewood and one of a hard, brittle wood. With his sticks he dug holes in the earth and planted each grain.   At twilight he had finished. After looking around to see that he had done every-thing properly, he walked to the west and camped among the foothills.

During the night he felt uneasy and began to wonder if someone else would claim the land. He determined to examine the surrounding country to see if he had any neighbors.

Next day he walked in a circle, sunwise, around the valley. He did this for four days, taking a wider circle each day, but met no one and saw no signs of human life. "It is good," he said, "No one claims the land before me."

On the fourth night, after his long day's walk around the valley, he sat by his fire facing the east. When darkness fell, he was surprised to see a faint gleam half way up the side of the mountains.

"Strange!" he exclaimed, "I have travelled all over that ground and have seen neither a man nor the remains of a fire."

Next morning Natinesthani set out to find the fire. When he reached the eastern mountain he found, what he had not observed before, a shelf in

the rocks, which seemed to run back some distance.
On the shelf he discovered two well-built huts.

The Navaho pushed aside the curtain of one of
the houses and saw, sitting inside, a young woman
making a fine buckskin shirt which she was deco-
rating with fringes and shells. Ashamed of his
ragged appearance, he hung his head and advanced,
looking at her under his eyebrows.

"Where are the men?" he asked and sat down
on the ground.

"My father and mother are in the other hut," she
replied carelessly.

Just as the Navaho had made up his mind to go
to the other house the father entered. "Why don't
you spread a skin for my son-in-law to sit on?" said
the old man to his daughter. She only smiled and
looked sideways at Natinesthani, who blushed.

The old man took a finely dressed Rocky Mountain sheepskin and a deerskin, spread them on the
ground beside the woman, and said to the stranger,
"Why do you not sit on the skins?"

Natinesthani made a motion as if to rise and take
the offered seat, but he sank back again in shame.
Invited a second time, he arose and sat down beside
the young woman.

When night came and they were alone together
she asked the Navaho his name. "I have two
names," he replied. "I am Natinesthani, He-Who-

Teaches-Himself, and I am Ahodiseli, He-Who-Has-Floated. Now you know my name you must tell me your father's."

"My father is called Deer-Raiser. I am Deer-Raiser's Daughter," the girl answered.

Natinesthani married Deer-Raiser's Daughter and stayed with her on the mountain. One morning he said to her, "I have a hut and a farm and a pet not far from here. I must go home today. Will you come with me?"

"Yes," agreed Deer-Raiser's Daughter, and went to her father to ask his permission. "My husband wants to go home now," she told him and the old man was annoyed.

"Tell him," Deer-Raiser said sharply, "that it is not the custom for a man to go so soon after his marriage. He should remain at least four days more."

The girl took this message back to Natinesthani and he slept that night in the lodge.

Next morning the young woman rose early. Soon after she had gone out the old man entered and said to the Navaho, "You do well to stay. My daughter and wife are preparing food for you. Don't go out until you have eaten."

The Indian made no reply. A little while after Deer-Raiser had left, his daughter returned, bringing a dish of stewed venison and a basketful of mush, which she silently handed to her husband.

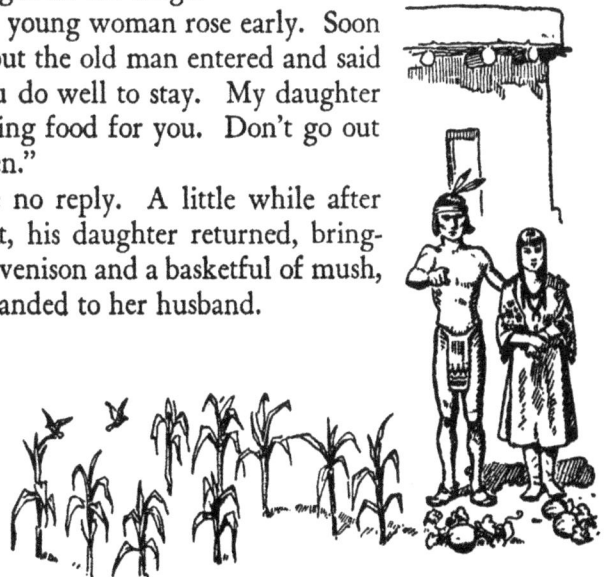

As he took the basket, Wind whispered in his ear, "There is poison mixed in the mush."

"Today, I may eat no mush," said Natinesthani. "The sun is already risen, and I have sworn that the sun shall never see me eat mush."

As the young woman passed out of the lodge with the remains of the meal, her father stopped her and asked, "How did my son-in-law eat this morning? Was he hungry?"

"He ate the stew, but would not touch the mush," she said.

"Ahahaha!" ejaculated the old man in a suspicious tone; but he said no more.

Again the Navaho stayed all day and all night.

The second morning, the young woman brought in, as usual, the venison stew and basket of mush. This time Wind whispered, "Don't touch the food. It is all poisoned."

"Wagh!" thought Natanesthani, "Deer-Raiser is a villainous wizard who would slay me. I shall have to flee for my life." He turned to his wife. "Pack your clothes," he bade her, "and be quick about it!"

Natinesthani and his wife fled swiftly down the steep trail together, and left the barren slopes of the mountain behind them.

Before long, they topped a little hill from which they could first see Natinesthani's field. It lay spread out below with the sun shining on it and the rain falling on it at the same time.   Above it was a dark cloud spanned by a rainbow.

When they reached the field, they strolled around it, and the Navaho pointed out many things. "This is my white corn, this is my blue corn, this is my yellow corn, and this is my corn of all colors. These we call squashes, these are melons, and these are beans," he said pointing to the various plants.

The bluebirds and yellowbirds were singing in the corn after the rain, and all was delightful to Deer-Raiser's Daughter.   She asked questions—how the seeds were planted, how the food was prepared and eaten. "These on the ground are melons; they are not ripe yet.   When they ripen we eat them raw," her husband explained.

He told her how the corn matured; how his people husked it and stored it for winter use, how they shelled, ground, and prepared it, and how they preserved some to sow in the spring.

Natinesthani and his wife moved into his hut on the farm by the whirling lake of Tonihilin, and with the pet turkey they dwell there still.

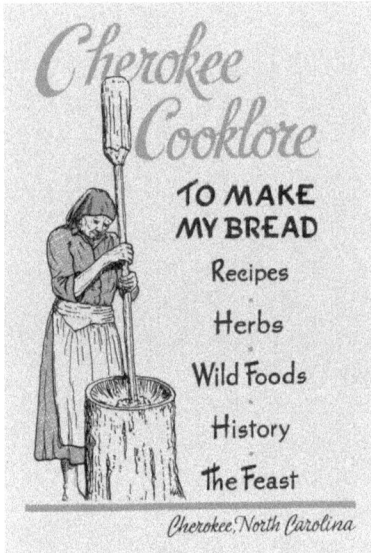

Cherokee Cooklore

TO MAKE MY BREAD

Recipes

Herbs

Wild Foods

History

The Feast

Cherokee, North Carolina

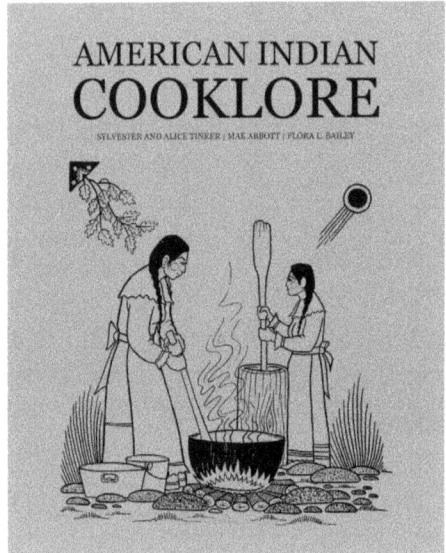

AMERICAN INDIAN
COOKLORE

SYLVESTER AND ALICE TINKER / MAE ABBOTT / FLORA L. BAILEY

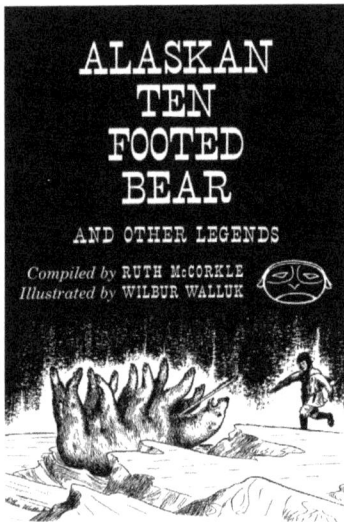

ALASKAN
TEN
FOOTED
BEAR

AND OTHER LEGENDS

Compiled by RUTH McCORKLE
Illustrated by WILBUR WALLUK

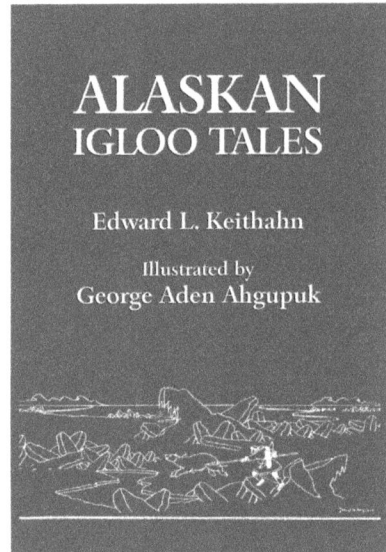

ALASKAN
IGLOO TALES

Edward L. Keithahn

Illustrated by
George Aden Ahgupuk

COACHWHIP PUBLICATIONS
COACHWHIPBOOKS.COM

THE SERPENT MOUND

E. O. RANDALL

THE RUBBER-BALL
GAMES OF THE
AMERICAS

THEODORE STERN

USHER L.
BURDICK

THE LAST DAYS OF
SITTING BULL
SIOUX MEDICINE CHIEF

KATHARINE LUOMALA
THE MENEHUNE
OF POLYNESIA
AND OTHER MYTHICAL LITTLE PEOPLE OF OCEANIA

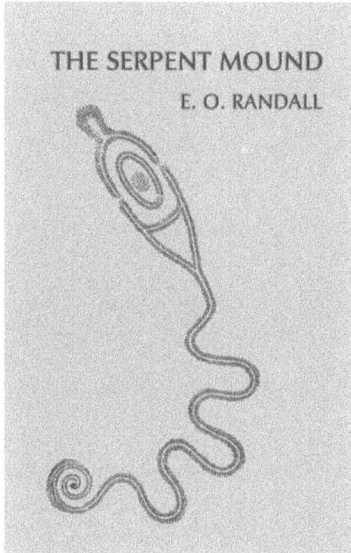

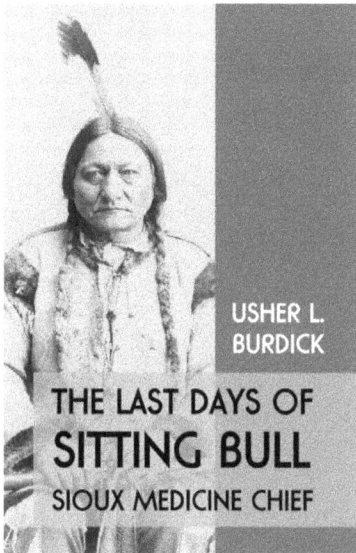

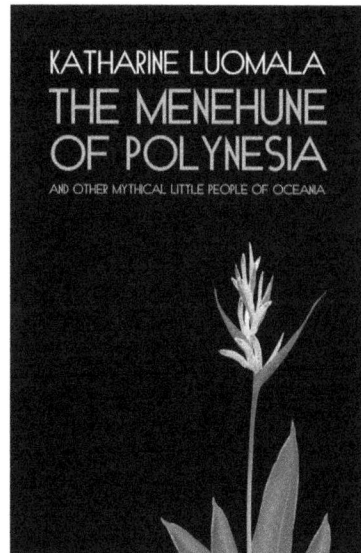

COACHWHIP PUBLICATIONS
COACHWHIPBOOKS.COM

www.ingramcontent.com/pod-product-compliance
Lightning Source LLC
Chambersburg PA
CBHW041429270326
41933CB00026B/3496